Teens and credit

At Issue

Teens and Credit

Other Books in the At Issue Series:

At Issue

| Teens and Credit

Roman Espejo, Book Editor

GREENHAVEN PRESS
A part of Gale, Cengage Learning

GALE
CENGAGE Learning™

Detroit • New York • San Francisco • New Haven, Conn • Waterville, Maine • London

Christine Nasso, *Publisher*
Elizabeth Des Chenes, *Managing Editor*

© 2010 Greenhaven Press, a part of Gale, Cengage Learning.

Gale and Greenhaven Press are registered trademarks used herein under license.

For more information, contact:
Greenhaven Press
27500 Drake Rd.
Farmington Hills, MI 48331-3535
Or you can visit our Internet site at gale.cengage.com

For product information and technology assistance, contact us at

Gale Customer Support, 1-800-877-4253
For permission to use material from this text or product, submit all requests online at www.cengage.com/permissions

Further permissions questions can be emailed to permissionrequest@cengage.com

Articles in Greenhaven Press anthologies are often edited for length to meet page requirements. In addition, original titles of these works are changed to clearly present the main thesis and to explicitly indicate the author's opinion. Every effort is made to ensure that Greenhaven Press accurately reflects the original intent of the authors. Every effort has been made to trace the owners of copyrighted material.

Cover image © Images.com/Corbis.

LIBRARY OF CONGRESS CATALOGING-IN-PUBLICATION DATA

Teens and credit / Roman Espejo, book editor.
     p. cm. -- (At issue)
    Includes bibliographical references and index.
    ISBN-13: 978-0-7377-4442-2 (hardcover)
    ISBN-13: 978-0-7377-4443-9 (pbk.)
    1. Credit cards--United States. 2. Credit--United States. 3. Teenagers--United States. 4. Finance, Personal--United States. I. Espejo, Roman, 1977-
    HG3755.8.U6T44 2009
    332.7'6508350973--dc22

                                     2009028938

Printed in the United States of America
1 2 3 4 5 6 7 13 12 11 10 09

Contents

Introduction

About ten percent of teenagers in the United States have a credit card, according to Teen Research Unlimited. Some teens, however, think their peers should leave home without them. Sean Pritchard, a high school senior in Macon, Georgia, speculates that credit cards provided by parents fail to impart financial literacy or responsibility. "For most teens," Pritchard claims, "they are given a credit card with their father's name on it with no spending limit and never see a single bill for anything they purchase."[1] Fellow Macon student Tyler Wilson offers a decidedly more negative opinion, "They suck your money out of your pocket, put you in debt, and you spend the rest of your life in a cardboard box."[2]

Nonetheless, many young cardholders count themselves among responsible spenders. "It's not too much of a responsibility if you use it appropriately and you don't rely on it,"[3] suggests Hannah Driver. Also hailing from Macon, the high school senior says her parents gave her a card for emergencies. As a matter of fact, some experts approve of such an arrangement. For example, youth Web site Family First Aid states, "Teen credit cards can be great tools in helping teach money management. If opened correctly, they can also help your teenager begin building credit."[4] Family First Aid advises parents to let their children deal with the consequences directly if they mishandle their finances, "If your teenager misses a payment, it is a good idea to revoke credit card privileges."[5] Likewise, numerous adults say they have benefited from signing up for credit early on. "Ultimately, my use of credit cards in

---

1. Lucy Ma, www.macon.com, April 28, 2009.
2. Lucy Ma, www.macon.com, April 28, 2009.
3. Lucy Ma, www.macon.com, April 28, 2009.
4. Family First Aid, www.familyfirstaid.org (accessed May 10, 2009).
5. Family First Aid, www.familyfirstaid.org (accessed May 10, 2009).

my teen years has resulted in me having a positive handle on my finances today,"[6] writes a commenter on FrugalDad.com.

Such contrasting opinions regarding credit cards often reflect differences in views about debt. Indeed, the average American is likely to take on debt during his or her lifetime. Some observers uphold that debt may be necessary, even beneficial. "Good debt includes anything you need but can't afford to pay for up front without wiping out cash reserves or liquidating all your investments,"[7] states CNNMoney.com. It identifies three types of "good debt": purchasing a home, buying a car, and financing a college education. "In fact, there are instances where the leveraging power of a loan actually helps put you in a better overall financial position,"[8] the Web site proposes. Financial journalist Karen Blumenthal concurs. "At times, we need to pay off a major purchase or medical bill over a few months," she contends. "Taking on some debt can sometimes really pay off . . ."[9] So-called good debt often is categorized as secured, which the Federal Trade Commission describes as "tied to an asset, like your car for a car loan, or your house for a mortgage."[10] Bad debt, of course, would cover most everything else. CNNMoney.com is quick to point out that this "includes debt you've taken on for things you don't need and can't afford (that trip to Bora Bora, for instance)."[11] Moreover, CNNMoney.com adds that charging through life with Visa, MasterCard, and other cards is the most risky kind of debt. "The worst form of debt is credit card debt, since it usually carries the highest interest rates,"[12] it claims. On the other hand, some commentators maintain

6. www.FrugalDad.com, March 25, 2009.
7. www.money.cnn.com (accessed May 10, 2009).
8. www.money.cnn.com (accessed May 10, 2009).
9. Yahoo! Finance, May 5, 2009.
10. www.ftc.gov, December 2005.
11. www.money.cnn.com (accessed May 10, 2009).
12. www.money.cnn.com (accessed May 10, 2009).

that *all* debt is bad debt. Dave Ramsey, a personal finance author and motivational speaker, argues, "Most normal people are just plain broke because they are in debt up to their eyeballs with no hope of help. If you're in debt, then you're a slave . . ."[13] He contests the proposed ability of debt to leverage major costs: "My contention is that debt brings on enough risk to offset any advantage that could be gained through leverage of debt. Given time—a lifetime—risk will destroy the perceived returns . . ."[14]

The opinion on teens and credit cards, then, is divided. The one in ten American teenagers who uses credit is perceived to be on the road to A) becoming fiscally savvy and building a solid credit history, or B) financial ruin and lifelong debt. In *At Issue: Teens and Credit*, the authors debate the advantages and disadvantages and opportunities and risks of giving young consumers the power of plastic.

13. www.daveramsey.com (accessed May 10, 2009).
14. www.daveramsey.com (accessed May 10, 2009).

1

Teens Should Have Credit Cards

Caren Weiner Campbell

Caren Weiner Campbell is a writer based in New York City.

More teens want the convenience of having their own credit or debit cards as the use of plastic becomes commonplace. Although the temptations of "swipe-and-sign" are ever-present, parents can choose from suitable and versatile card options for their children. From debit cards linked to their bank accounts to rechargeable prepaid cards to joint credit cards, each choice presents its own costs and risks as well as conveniences and benefits. Combined with parental supervision and teachable moments about spending, credit and debit cards can help teens become financially responsible while establishing solid credit histories.

We're living on a plastic planet, where even vending machines, parking meters and Starbucks branches are now accepting credit and debit cards for everyday transactions. It's no wonder that teens hanker for their own charge cards, considering that the average 15- to 18-year-old spends $2,600 a year on discretionary items alone, according to a 2008 study by Piper Jaffrey, an investment bank and research firm.

"Getting a credit card is a rite of passage," says Todd Mark, vice president of education for Consumer Credit Counseling Service, or CCCS, of Greater Dallas.

In fact, a 2009 study by Sallie Mae reveals that 39 percent of college freshmen obtained their first credit card while still in high school, compared to just 23 percent in 2004. And of course, college freshmen get bombarded with credit card come-ons as soon as they set foot on campus. By the end of their freshman year, students average $2,038 in credit card debt and a staggering 23 percent have four or more credit cards, according to the Sallie Mae study.

Facing this prospect, plenty of debt-dubious parents wonder how best to introduce kids to the temptations of swipe-and-sign. As with most child-rearing decisions, the best course of action depends on the individual child. But thanks to an ever-increasing number of credit and debit options, savvy grown-ups can choose the card best suited to a teen's temperament, financial sophistication and maturity level.

Starting Out

Youngsters who already have a checking or savings account—and that should be the first step in a kid's financial education—are ready for a standard debit card because they're accustomed to keeping track of transactions, according to Marc Minker, a certified public accountant and managing director at the New York City public accounting firm Mahoney Cohen & Co.

Getting a credit card is a rite of passage.

Parents can rest fairly easy in this situation since even the most acquisitive teen will find it self-limiting: Once the account balance drops to zero, theoretically, he or she has to stop spending.

And conveniently, many employers will deposit wages directly into a teen's account.

However, since a debit card is taking money from a checking or savings account, overdrafts and the resulting fees can add up quickly. What's more, if junior's money gets debited via fraud or error, or if there is a problem with a merchant, recouping the already-gone cash can be difficult.

The Fair Credit Billing Act has different rules for liability with debit card fraud or theft. If you report the card missing before the thief makes any transactions, the issuer can't hold you liable for any charges. If you report the loss within two business days, you will be responsible only for $50 of charges. If you don't report the loss within 60 days, you can be liable for $500 of transactions. These rules make it important to check the account regularly to be sure there are no problems. However, debit cards from a major card issuer such as Visa or MasterCard carry the same fraud protections as credit cards, with zero liability.

Prepaid Cards Have One Major Drawback

If this setup gives you nightmares of your teen debiting away his college funds, you, and he or she, might be better off with a prepaid card or stored-value card. Not linked to a bank account, this variation on the debit card—Visa Buxx is a well-known example—sets even firmer limitations on spending. Parents activate the card by loading it with an appropriate amount of money. Other authorized adults, such as Uncle Joe or grandma, can also add funds for birthdays or Christmas or when they see fit. Then mom, dad and the teenager can keep an eye on expenditures via online statements. "Stored-value cards are basically cash," says Mark, "so they're easy for kids to understand."

As a result, it's no surprise that stored-value cards are marketed overwhelmingly toward the teen demographic, and each uses a slightly different marketing angle.

MasterCard's affinity-based MYPlash features images of pop musicians, rockers and athletes, while hip-hop mogul Russell Simmons' RushCard offers tie-ins with mobile phones and discounts on clothing from his Phat Farm line and his ex-wife's Baby Phat label. Paychecks can also be deposited onto the RushCard.

The Allow Card, a MasterCard-branded prepaid card, aims to educate teen cardholders by e-mailing them a monthly "financial lesson." It also offers parents 35 controls, including the ability to block certain types of merchants so that teens can't shop at undesirable places.

MasterCard-branded PAYjr operates on the allowance principle: Parents deposit a teen's allowance onto a PAYjr card, and parent and teen can monitor use online. For kids 12 and younger, PAYjr has a savings program tied to chores: Parents set up a list of chores and due dates; once the chores are completed, the payment is automatically deposited into a savings account. UPside card, a Visa-allied card, is a prepaid card that can be used online, in stores and at ATMs. It also has a points program that allows users to get cash back.

All of these stored-value cards have one major drawback: Just about every action entails a fee. For example, U.S. Bank charges its Buxx customers for enrollment, balance inquiries, reloading or replacing the card, and assistance from a bank teller. And here's the one-two punch: If you don't use your card for a few weeks or months, you'll get socked with an "inactivity fee."

The Allow Card has a $19.95 activation and "lifetime membership" fee, and fees for ATM withdrawals ($1.50), monthly maintenance ($3.50), balance inquiry at points of sale ($0.25), and others. There are no fees for point-of-sale purchases.

Revolving Credit

"The basic principles of spending money come long before the first credit card," says Mark. "There's a whole collection of related topics: the value of a dollar, the time value of money, interest (and) the idea of saving toward a purchase." Armed with that understanding, teens are ready to graduate to credit cards—something they should do before graduating from high school, according to personal finance experts.

Establishing Healthy Habits

"People have to learn this stuff sometime," says John Parfrey, director of the High School Financial Planning Program for the National Endowment for Financial Education, or NEFE. "Managing credit is all about establishing those healthy habits and patterns early."

Mark agrees.

"If you're letting your kid (who is) under 18 use a credit card, make sure you're teaching them the skills of spending and then paying off in full immediately," he says. "That's Credit 101."

There are three ways to go: You can get a joint credit card, which means you and your child are jointly responsible for the debt; you can get a secured credit card, which is tied to the teen's savings account; or you can make your teen an authorized user, which means you, not your child, are responsible for the debt.

As a first foray into credit, Minker recommends a low-limit joint credit card in the teen's name, backed by a co-signing parent. A person younger than 18 cannot apply for a credit card without a parent's approval, so this is a good way for a parent to monitor a teen's card use while building a credit history for the teen.

Though the joint arrangement allows parents to keep a rein on the card's limit, junior should be responsible for paying the bill in full. "That forces him to start thinking about having enough money set aside by the end of the month," Minker says.

Once the statement arrives, or whenever you track card activity online, he says, "sit down with your kid for 10 minutes and go over what was spent." Ideally, he says, "the teen wouldn't be using the card for clothing or food; it'd be used in case of an emergency, or to finally buy something they've been saving up for."

Mark says, "They shouldn't be using it as a short-term loan or as a way to leverage their lifestyle."

All of this training is undercut, however, if parents "swoop in and save the kid" from the consequences of overspending, says Minker. "I'd much rather have my daughter fall on her face while she's under my roof—but if I bail her out every time, that sends the wrong message."

Another option is a secured credit card tied to the teen's savings account. The card's limit is usually equal to the teen's savings account balance. If the teen misses a monthly payment, the bank takes it from the savings account. This type of card also helps build a credit history. The downside of a secured card is that the annual percentage rate, or APR, of interest is relatively high, between 13 percent and 24 percent. Credit unions often have lower APRs, so it's worth shopping around.

Finally, there's the option of making your teen an authorized user of your credit card. It's convenient, it's easy, it's commonly done—but it could result in a "megasplurge," potentially putting your budget, and good credit score, at risk. Here again, "supervision is the key," says Minker.

Jittery parents can ... take heart from surveys showing that many kids understand the pitfalls of plastic.

Good Debt v. Bad Debt

As with the joint card, parents need to review and discuss monthly credit card statements with their teen, says CCCS's Mark, and all parties should be monitoring expenses. "The kid should be keeping track of all his or her spending rather than waiting to be told at the end of the month what he owes."

When a parent authorizes a teenage child to use a card, the credit bureaus will report the use of that card under the parent's name as well as the teen's name. This enables the teen to establish a credit history by piggybacking on the parent's good credit history. And the reverse is true as well: If a parent has a poor credit history, the teen will start his or her financial life with a poor credit history. Because children under the age of 18 can't legally enter into a contract, the parent is the one who's legally responsible for the debt.

With a joint card, the teen's actions are more likely to accrue to her own nascent credit record. That's the good news and the bad news. "There is a danger of a teen getting off on the wrong foot with their credit rating if the kid is not well-trained and uses the card unwisely," says Minker.

To that end, jittery parents can also take heart from surveys showing that many kids understand the pitfalls of plastic. In a 2008 GfK Roper Survey commissioned by Bankrate, 60 percent of 18- to 24-year-olds strongly agreed with the statement "Credit cards make it too easy for American consumers to spend more than they earn."

"Teens are getting the message that credit has a down side," says Parfrey. "But since debt is inevitable, we emphasize the idea of creditworthiness—good debt versus bad debt. After all, it's important to have an established credit record and credit scores. When you buy a house, it's not as if you can just put down cash on the barrelhead."

2

Teens Should Not Have Credit Cards

Janet Bodnar

Janet Bodnar is editor of Kiplinger's Personal Finance *magazine and author of* Dollars and Sense for Kids.

Giving children and teens credit or debit cards is not the way to teach financial responsibility, because they will get hooked on plastic. Cards geared toward teens are marketing gimmicks that encourage shopping and give young consumers a direct line to their parents' cash. Instead, a child should spend money only from an allowance, and teens should obtain debit cards only after securing a part-time job. Furthermore, it is recommended that young adults postpone getting credit cards until after college graduation, when they have gained experience in managing money and when they presumably have grasped the distinctions among the different types of charge accounts.

Not long ago, I was asked to appear on a TV show to discuss whether youngsters should carry credit cards. "What's to discuss?" I asked the producer. "That's the dumbest idea I've ever heard." Not so fast, I was told. Some people think that if kids use credit cards when they're still at home, they will handle credit responsibly when they're on their own.

I repeat: It's the dumbest idea I've ever heard. Giving your kids credit cards is like letting them use drugs early so that they won't turn into addicts. I'm all for learning to use credit responsibly, but a card to practice on isn't the way to do it.

The best way to teach kids to manage credit is to have them start with cold, hard cash—cold and hard being the operative words. Spending money is more real to kids, even teenagers, when they have to count out the bills and look down into an empty wallet. As my 16-year-old son puts it, "If I don't have cash, I can't buy stuff I don't need. If have a credit card, I can buy anything."

That's what makes a new marketing gimmick like the Hello Kitty Debit MasterCard so insidious. Like the Visa Buxx card, which has been around a while, Hello Kitty is a prepaid card aimed at children. Parents are encouraged to get the card for girls as young as 10 and reload it with cash when it's empty. The card, which is also loaded with fees, can be used to make purchases or get cash out of an ATM. Purchases can be tracked online, and pushers of this plastic promote it as a way to help kids learn to manage finances.

Giving your kids credit cards is like letting them use drugs early so that they won't turn into addicts.

But kids won't get it. To them, plastic is magic money. Credit cards, debit cards, prepaid cards—you name it they're all just a direct line to Mom and Dad's wallet. In one survey, 35% of teens said having a prepaid cash card would make them "look cooler in front of their friends."

Shopper's Paradise

What card issuers really want to do is get plastic into little hands so kids can buy stuff, online and elsewhere (Hello Kitty bills itself as the "cutest way to shop"). To get Moms and Dads to buy into this, one of the creators of the Hello Kitty card told the *Washington Post* that parents can monitor where their daughters spend money: "You get a higher level of control than if you just gave your daughter $100 and said, 'Go to the mall.'"

But parents have even more control if they insist their children finance mall excursions out of their own earnings or allowance, which I define as a fixed amount of money that kids get at regular intervals to pay for agreed-upon expenses. I've got nothing against kids buying stuff—as long as they don't hit up their parents for $20 to $100 every time they head out the door.

Life Lessons

That's not to say you shouldn't discuss credit with high schoolers. But instead of lecturing them, use a quick, interactive example, such as an online calculator (like the one at kiplinger.com/tools) to show them how long it can take to pay off a credit-card bill.

Once teens have learned to handle cash, they can start to use plastic in ways that make sense. For example, when they get a part-time job, help them open a checking account with an ATM or debit card so they can deposit, withdraw and spend their own money.

College students don't need credit cards, either. "I had a gasoline card for emergencies," one young woman confessed, "and my roommate and I always used it to buy food at the gas-station convenience store." The time to apply for credit is shortly before they graduate, after they've had experience managing money for several years and can appreciate the distinctions among the various cards. When I recently drove my college-senior son back to school, he and I had a long talk about when to use a credit versus a debit card—a discussion my 16-year-old would not have the patience for.

3

Teens Offer Risks as Customers for Credit Card Companies

Danielle Gorman

Danielle Gorman is a contributor to American Banker, *a print and Web publication for banking and financial services professionals.*

The teen and student markets for credit cards are growing and may offer credit card companies opportunities to foster lifelong brand loyalty among young people. Nonetheless, pursuing these inexperienced cardholders is risky. Young people may be hungry consumers, but credit card companies and banks may become burdened by teens' inability to manage or pay off debts. Moreover, customer turnover is high, and teens are usually issued limited amounts of credit that do not generate substantial revenue. Therefore, credit card companies and banks are better off courting the teen market with prepaid and debit cards rather than credit cards.

Banks that market credit cards to teenagers and college students must weigh the potential for gaining lifelong customers against the obvious risks of lending to people with little experience managing their finances.

The number of teens who use credit cards rises each year, and as the age at which card use begins continues to drop, critics say targeting this demographic can do banks more harm than good. However, some banks are trying to sign up teens for prepaid debit cards, which they tout as a way to help young people learn to budget.

Despite the ongoing credit crunch, 10.4% of teens said they used credit cards this year, up from 8.5% last year, according to a survey released in May [2008] by JA Worldwide, a nonprofit that promotes financial knowledge among elementary and high school students. (Eighteen- and 19-year-olds may have credit cards in their own name, while 16- and 17-year-olds often have a co-signer. Younger teens may be authorized users of their parents' cards.)

Susan Menke, a senior financial services analyst at the market research firm Mintel International Group Ltd., said it is hard to tell whether banks are more actively pursuing this market, since credit card mail solicitations are down overall this year.

Young-adult Cards

A search of Mintel's database found 52 issuers that targeted students through print, direct mail, and e-mail advertisements between January and June [2008]. A search for the same period in 2006 returned 72 issuers. However, Ms. Menke said, "the student market is huge" and of "increasing interest."

Frontier Bank in Park City, Utah, is one of at least half a dozen issuers of the Visa Buxx prepaid debit card. Vivian Arriaga, the bank's central operations manager in Palm Desert, Calif. (where it does business as El Paseo Bank), said the strategic rationale for marketing to teens is that "the earlier you start, the better" it is for fostering brand loyalty.

"We want to be the first impression children have of banks," she said.

Similarly, U.S. Bancorp's Elan Financial Services, which offers a Young Adult Visa Classic credit card, says on its Web site: "Research shows that cardholders will likely remain loyal to the issuer of their first credit card."

The card is available to anyone 16 and older with a co-signer and marketed as a way for young adults to establish a credit rating. Elan also issues the College Rewards Visa Card, which does not require a co-signer and lets students earn points toward electronics and entertainment discounts. Elan declined to comment for this article. (U.S. Bancorp also issues a Visa Buxx card.)

Capital One Financial Corp. offers four "young adult" cards for people 18 and older with little or no credit history. Diana Don, a spokeswoman for the McLean, Va., issuer, said credit lines on these cards range from $300 to $3,000. She would not say how many people have applied for or received the cards, and referred other questions to the card networks.

Less Responsible Cardholders

The JA Worldwide survey found that 13.2% of the 72 respondents who used cards paid only the minimum balance each month. Judge John C. Ninfo 2nd, of the U.S. Bankruptcy Court for the Western District of New York, said teens who have not learned the basics of personal finance may easily fall into lifelong debt.

Banks would be best off not aggressively pursuing the teen market.

"These customers aren't as responsible—they're hungry consumers," said Mr. Ninfo, who founded Credit Abuse Resistance Education, a national program funded by the bankruptcy court. "The longer we can keep credit cards out of their hands, probably the better."

C. Red Gillen, a senior analyst at the research firm Celent, a Marsh & McLennan Cos. unit, said that if a high percentage of teens have difficulty managing the debt they run up on their credit cards, "it will blow up in the bank's face."

"I think that given the amount of 'churn' in the credit card space, there are very few lifelong customers," Mr. Gillen said. "Combine this with the fact that teens typically aren't issued a very large line of credit—and thus don't represent a huge revenue opportunity—and I think banks would be best off not aggressively pursuing the teen market." (The survey found that 38% of teen cardholders charge an average of $50 or less a month.) If banks seek lifelong customers, it is more "prudent and responsible" for them to offer debit or prepaid cards, he said.

Such prepaid products include the MYplash issued by First Premier Bank of Sioux Falls, S.D., whose users receive exclusive offers from musical artists; and the PAYjr card issued by MetaBank of Storm Lake, Iowa, which lets parents transfer money into children's accounts once they have finished assigned chores.

The Visa Buxx card is available to those 13 and older and can store up to $250. "The core of the product is about financial responsibility, and teaching young adults to properly use payment products," said Steve Diamond, Visa Inc.'s senior business leader of prepaid products. The card is valuable to the network and its issuers because teens are a "huge demographic with a lot of spending power."

El Paseo often markets the card to parents, but also brings students into branches to learn about saving. Haddon Libby, the bank's chief financial officer, said these visits are often the child's first introduction to a financial institution, and that most who visit choose to open a savings account or get a Visa Buxx card. Many of the children remain with the bank after their under-18 account expires and open a checking account, Mr. Libby said.

4

Parent-supervised Credit Cards Can Help Teens Build Credit

Nancy Trejos

Nancy Trejos is a columnist for the Washington Post.

According to a 2007 survey, only 45 percent of teens know how to use credit cards and just 26 percent understand credit card interest and other fees. With parental supervision, however, credit and debit cards can teach children financial literacy. Giving teens credit cards enables parents to help them at home when they make financial mistakes—rather than trying to manage such problems remotely when young people are away at college. Credit cards also can give teens an early start on building good credit. However, teens may be unable to secure approval for their own credit cards. And if a parent and child obtain a joint card, mismanagement on either end can damage both credit records. For this reason, prepaid cards are a less risky way to help teens graduate from paper to plastic.

Shashi Bellamkonda would like his 16-year-old daughter to get a credit card as soon as she is eligible.

Okay, that might sound kind of dangerous considering how much we have heard about teenagers (and let's face it, adults) getting into trouble with credit cards. Aren't there members of Congress who want to ban credit card companies from marketing to college students and young people in general? (The answer is yes.)

Bellamkonda, a 45-year-old Potomac resident who devises social media strategy for a company in Reston, understands that. But he considers his daughter Mitali, a high school junior with good grades, responsible enough to handle credit. And he wants her to establish a credit history. After all, aren't we all supposed to take on a little bit of debt early in our lives in order to qualify for that good debt, such as a mortgage, later on in life?

There's another reason Bellamkonda wants his daughter to have a credit card. He wants it to be a learning experience. She's young enough now that if she has access to a credit card, he can monitor it. He'd rather she not have her first experience with credit when she is far away or living alone.

"Youngsters need to know that this is not a bottomless pit. So this may help educate her," he said. "Our prime focus should be on teaching children how to work with these various instruments."

If she makes mistakes, so be it, he said. "I'm not saying I want her to make mistakes, but if she does, it would be a good experience because we will be there to help her," he said.

Bellamkonda is wondering: Is this a good strategy? How should parents go about teaching their children about credit cards? Can his daughter even get a credit card? If so, would he be able to monitor the balance?

The credit card experts I consulted applauded Bellamkonda for teaching his daughter financial literacy early in life. Emily Peters, a personal finance expert for Credit.com, points to a 2007 Charles Schwab survey that showed that only 45 percent of teens know how to use a credit card. Even worse, just 26 percent of teens understood credit card interest and fees. "Shashi's doing the right thing by making sure she'll be prepared for her credit future," Peters said.

But there are a few things Bellamkonda should consider before letting his daughter enter credit territory.

First of all, she might not even be able to get her own credit card. The recession has made financial institutions squeamish about giving unsecured loans, which is what credit cards are, to people with no established credit history. If she is able to get a credit card, he would probably have to be a co-signer, which means that if she mismanages the account, his credit score would be damaged along with hers.

Many personal finance experts would urge against letting your children get their own credit cards until they have a job that allows them to pay off their balances. Some even say they should wait until after college.

In the meantime, Bellamkonda has other, much better, options. If the goal is to get her used to dealing with plastic rather than cash, he can get her a debit card or a prepaid card with a low limit, say $250. Curtis Arnold, founder of CardRatings.com, said there are prepaid cards targeted specifically at teens, such as the Visa Buxx card. With such a card, Bellamkonda would be able to log in and monitor his daughter's spending online, Arnold said.

Getting a teenager a credit card while she lives in your home is a great teaching opportunity on finances.

Arnold had his son, who just turned 18, start with a debit card. "I will definitely encourage my son to get a credit card when he gets in college after he has proven to me that he can use a debit card without any issues," he said.

Peters said Bellamkonda could also add his daughter as an authorized user on one of his existing accounts. That would allow him to monitor her spending. If she spends too much, he could pull the plug.

"That way, she'll gain the experience of using credit and start building her credit history but will not be legally responsible for her own account yet," Peters said.

Of course, if Bellamkonda's credit is bad and he doesn't properly manage the card, his daughter's credit file would be damaged. But that does not appear to be the case.

Whatever he decides to do, Bellamkonda should have a long, honest talk with his daughter.

Show her how carrying a balance and making minimum payments can result in finance charges far greater than the original purchase amount. CardRatings.com has an online calculator that illustrates this point. There are also good financial literacy resources at Jumpstart.org.

Bill Hardekopf, chief executive of LowCards.com, said parents should pull out their own credit card bills and talk their children through them. Explain the interest rate, minimum payments, grace period and finance charges. If they've had late fees or payment problems, they shouldn't hide them. "Use these as teaching examples," he said. "Getting a teenager a credit card while she lives in your home is a great teaching opportunity on finances."

5

Prepaid Debit Cards for Teens Are an Alternative to Credit Cards

Joseph Kenny

Joseph Kenny is webmaster of the card-comparison Web site Credit Card Web, which is based in the United Kingdom.

The allure of easy spending and access to extravagant purchases leads many credit cardholders to live beyond their means. Likewise, teens may neither resist the pull of plastic nor have the financial know-how needed to use credit cards sensibly. Prepaid credit cards, on the other hand, are a viable alternative. The lack of interest charges and overdraft fees and the ability to limit and track spending are among the advantages for young, inexperienced cardholders. However, to effectively teach money management, parents must enforce budget restrictions and not recharge cards whenever their children run out of credit.

Credit cards are *en vogue* even if the results of using such fashionable payment methods are less than stylish. This isn't stopping the millions of consumers who use a credit card for purchases ranging from the mundane to the extravagant. The next generation of consumers, teenagers, is seeing the allure of the quick and easy purchases that can be made even if it's not affordable, and [the generation] wants desperately to be part of it.

Credit cards allow a lifestyle that may otherwise be impossible. Even though the repercussions of living beyond your means is nothing but stress and hardship, consumers are more than willing to take part in the facade. Teenagers look upon this as status quo and strive to reach it the same way their parents have; through credit cards.

Teens and credit cards are never a good idea. Many teenagers are not versed in the responsibility needed to use a card wisely much like most of their parents. When and if a teen receives a credit card, they are not prone to think ahead to how they will repay the loan and what will happen if they fail to do so. A solution that is quickly becoming popular with both teens and parents is the prepaid credit card, which is offered through many credit card companies.

The prepaid credit card works much the same way as a gift card. The parent will load money onto the card, which then can be used at any retail or merchant that accepts the credit card company that issued the prepaid card. There are several benefits to using such a card, including:

- Convenience

- Security

- A lesson in budgeting

- Parents can track spending habits

- The cards have overdraft protection

- A limit is placed on spending

- No Overdraft fees

- No Interest charges

A Great Tool

Parents feel secure giving their teens a prepaid credit card knowing that the kid will only be able to spend up to the limit on the card. This fact attracts parents and their teens to the prepaid credit cards; there is no risk of spending more than you can afford. Many who oppose the cards claim that this benefit is also a major pitfall that shows teens that there is no accountability when using a credit card.

While prepaid credit cards are not exactly the same thing as credit cards, they can be used just the same.

Parents need to actively teach their children responsible money management, including budgeting to avoid any misconception or confusion. When allocating money to the card, parents should be firm and tell the teen that once the money is gone, it is gone. There is no such thing as a free lunch. Many parents are using prepaid cards in place of cash allowances for the ease and convenience. Not only this, but parents will be able to monitor their child's spending habits online in monthly statements. This gives them an added sense of security knowing what the money is going towards.

While prepaid credit cards are not exactly the same thing as credit cards, they can be used just the same. By granting a prepaid card, parents will be able to teach their teens valuable financial lessons that will, hopefully, translate over to the real world. Teens with credit cards are irresponsible and are known to rack up an amazing amount of debt in a very short time. By showing them how quickly money can disappear, the prepaid cards teach teens responsible spending habits and demonstrate that those charges have to be paid off somehow.

It's up to the parents to stick with a firm plan if they are going to give a teen a prepaid credit card. You can not fill it up every time the teen spends the entire amount that was placed on the card. Set a monthly limit and explain to your child that once the money is gone, then they will just have to wait until next month. If you want to take it a step further, allow the teen to borrow money and take that amount from next month's total. You may also want to have your teen work for the money through chores or at the family business until they get a job on their own.

Prepaid credit cards can be a great option for parents who do not want their teenagers to have access to a credit card. Used responsibly and in conjunction with financial education, these prepaid credit cards are a great tool for the preparation of the real world.

6

Many Teens Do Not Want Credit Cards

Jennifer Alsever

Jennifer Alsever is a writer based in Denver, Colorado.

Fewer of today's teens are interested in getting credit cards. Other forms of plastic, debit and prepaid cards, now fill their wallets. In addition, youth financial planning classes and well-known stories of college students amassing loads of debt have tempered teens' appetite for credit. Still, young shoppers wield family spending influence and increasing purchasing power. In response, credit card companies and banks have created lines of prepaid cards, some featuring celebrities, for teens and pre-teenagers. And plastic is still cool among image-conscious teens whose parents have allowed them to have credit cards.

Teenagers are a fickle bunch: first they wanted credit cards of their own and now it seems they don't.

That is not to say they avoid all plastic. These days, their wallets are full of other cards, including debit cards, which draw money from banking accounts, and a wealth of prepaid cards that store a certain cash value that can be tapped with a swipe of the card.

Just 15 percent of teenagers surveyed this spring said that they were interested in obtaining a credit card in their own name, down from 34 percent surveyed in 2000, according to a survey of 2,000 teenagers conducted by Teenage Research Unlimited, a market research firm in Northbrook, Ill.

The portion who have credit cards in their name also declined, to 9 percent of teenagers from 11 percent in 2000. Children under the age of 18 cannot legally apply for their own credit cards, but parents can co-sign for them.

The lack of enthusiasm may stem in part from these new forms of plastic as well as from the influx of financial planning classes geared toward youth and the well-publicized stories of college students drowning in debt, said Rob Callender, trends director for Teenage Research Unlimited. The average college undergraduate has $2,169 in credit card debt, according to a 2005 report by the student lender Nellie Mae.

Teenagers are a fickle bunch: first they wanted credit cards of their own and now it seems they don't.

"I wouldn't be surprised if this data shows they've learned from mistakes of the past and they aren't willing to make the same mistakes in the future," Mr. Callender said. "This group of teens has a great head on their shoulders. They're driven. They're motivated. They're savvy."

They are also experienced shoppers who wield increasing influence in America's discretionary spending. In 2004, the nation's 33 million teenagers, ages 12 to 19, accounted for $169 billion in spending—not including spending on their behalf or family purchases they may have influenced, according to Teenage Research Unlimited. Much of that money bought clothing, snacks, shoes, CDs, video games, MP3 players, computer equipment and cellphones.

The spending has not gone unnoticed by card companies and banks. MasterCard has recently introduced a prepaid card called MyPlash, a reloadable debit card that can be stocked with a limited amount of cash. The card has pictures of music celebrities like Clay Aiken, appealing to young consumers.

Visa also has prepaid cards, including a Hilary Duff Visa and the Visa Buxx card tailored to preteenagers. Card companies emphasize that the cards are not credit cards and so can better prepare youth for the day they sign up for their own credit card.

"It requires teens to live within a budget," said Rhonda Bentz, spokeswoman for Visa USA in San Francisco. She said parents could limit spending and easily monitor where money goes, while still ensuring that their children have money when traveling or in case of emergencies.

"Doling out cash is more antiquated," said Jenifer Lippincott of Weston, Mass., who automatically transfers weekly allowances into checking accounts for her two daughters, ages 14 and 16, who pay for most entertainment with their debit cards. Ms. Lippincott said the system required her children to keep track of their balances and left a neat audit trail of spending.

And, given the current climate of repeated data corruption and fears of identity theft, she is happy her teenagers are opting for alternatives to credit cards.

"When I hear about these things, my immediate reaction is phew," said, Ms. Lippincott, who also wrote the book, "Seven Things Your Teenager Won't Tell You (And How to Talk About Them Anyway)" published by Ballantine Books this year. "With debit cards, you are really getting the best of both worlds. The teen can have the experience of having a credit card without the liability."

She said her 16-year-old, Anabel, got her debit card at age 15, and her youngest daughter, Tess, got her card even younger, at 13. Tess, now 14, said she liked her card because her money was always easily accessible for movies or eating out. Plus, she said, "it makes me feel more grown up."

Not everyone views prepaid and debit cards for teenagers so positively.

"It's the last frontier for credit card companies trying to expand their markets," said Jim Tehan, spokesman for

Myvesta.org, a Rockville, Md., nonprofit consumer education organization. "They're looking younger and younger because if they can get that first card in their hands, they're a customer for life."

A MasterCard spokeswoman, Barbara Coleman, disputed that assertion. "We don't market to kids," she said, adding that MYplash was aimed at fans of the celebrity pictured on the front of the card. Still, she said, parents could use the cards to teach children about managing finances.

Critics, however, worry about teenagers developing bad habits, especially when it comes to accumulating debt.

"The money is just abstract," said James A. Roberts, a marketing professor at Baylor University in Waco, Tex., who has spent 10 years studying credit card behavior. People who use credit cards tend to spend more, are less price-sensitive and overestimate their wealth, he said.

For years, card companies have been criticized for aggressive pitches to college students and offers of free T-shirts and other perks for opening accounts. Some colleges banned card companies from campuses because of concern that students would pile up heavy debts.

Ben Marvin saw the college credit card problem firsthand, as media manager at the College of Saint Rose in Albany. He decided then that at his household, credit cards would be forbidden entirely. His two daughters, now 18 and 25, can qualify on their own for credit, but they still do not have cards.

"They needed to learn that money isn't ephemeral. It's real," Mr. Marvin said. "They needed to get the feel of money going into their hands and out of their hands. With credit cards, it's too easy."

Mr. Marvin's youngest daughter, Johanna, now a freshman at Butler University in Indianapolis, said she did not mind her parents' rule.

"I would not be responsible enough to handle it, knowing when to use it, when to not, paying the bills," she said. "I try to keep cash on me. You never know when you're going to need it."

Credit cards have not disappeared from teenage life entirely. At 15, Emily Merkel of Portland, Ore., was not old enough to drive a car, but she was charging clothes, dinners and online music to her own credit card, a birthday gift from her parents with few spending restrictions beyond the card's $1,000 limit.

"There aren't many rules, I guess," said Ms. Merkel, now 16. "Just don't spend money you don't have. Pay your bill every month."

Ms. Merkel sometimes keeps a note in her purse with her card balance, so she knows what she is spending. The monthly bill arrives addressed to her mother, who hands it to Ms. Merkel to pay with her allowance from a checking account. She said she was glad to have the early training before going off to college. She said that credit card payments were easy to make using the Internet.

"I have never overspent," Ms. Merkel said. "There are people I know who have abused a credit card. But I find it really helpful. I'm not a big cash person. If I have cash, I'm tempted to spend it."

And at some high schools, credit cards still remain cool.

"Having a credit card in high school was about proving yourself, your image," said Jessie Evangelista of Cherrytown, N.Y., who obtained her own card in ninth grade as a reward for earning good grades. Now 19, she is a freshman at Middlebury College in Middlebury, Vt.

Tips for Teaching Children to Use Credit, Debit or Prepaid Cards Wisely

Be a role model. Use your cards the way you want your children to use cards. Let children see you paying bills and hear discussions of how you spend your money. Be honest about spending mistakes of the past.

Help children learn the limits of their card. Go through monthly statements. Teach children about interest rates and how they can raise debt.

If your children receive an allowance, encourage them to budget, save and spend their money wisely, showing how interest charges, annual fees and bank charges work.

Set up long-term financial goals. Guide them to identify how they are spending their money and whether purchases are wise.

Instruct children what to do if a card is lost or stolen. Remind your children to keep the 800 number to report lost or stolen cards in a safe place. Urge them to memorize their secret PIN's and tell them not to lend cards.

Be aware of warning signs of identity theft, such as preapproved credit card offers arriving in your child's name.

Check your child's credit report annually for any unauthorized accounts and requests for credit.

7

Schools Should Educate Teens in Financial Literacy

Braun Mincher

Braun Mincher is author of The Secrets of Money: A Guide for Everyone on Practical Financial Literacy.

Even though most people make financial decisions and transactions on a regular basis, most teens in the United States do not learn basic personal finance in schools. The mortgage and stock market crises of 2008 underscore the importance of financial literacy. And a recent online survey reveals that the average American may not know the fundamentals, including how annual percentage rates (APR) work and the scope of required paycheck deductions. To help students succeed in a global economy, schools must teach personal finance alongside math and reading skills. Consumers also should educate themselves about financial matters and seek the guidance of a trusted coach or advisor.

Why does the school system require classes such as math, English, and science, but not basic personal finance?

We force students to learn trigonometry, yet how many of us ever use it again after graduation? In contrast, how many transactions involving money will we each conduct on a daily basis for the rest of our lives?

Think about each time you purchase something with a credit card, make a car payment, reconcile your bank account, or pay taxes. Even though these transactions are a daily occurrence for most consumers, we receive very little financial education on them from our school system, or even our parents.

Now think about how huge a decision it is to rent or purchase a home, apply for a loan or mortgage, make a contribution to your IRA or 401(k), shop for insurance, or get married. How do we expect to make wise financial decisions when we have little education on even the basics?

According to a 2007 survey commissioned by the National Council on Economic Education, only seven states currently require high school students to receive financial education in the school system. What about the other 43 states?

We need look no further than the daily news headlines about the mortgage meltdown, the stock market crisis, the housing slump, or the rising cost of oil to see how relevant financial literacy is.

Rather than waiting for the system to correct itself, we need to educate our future generations to make smarter financial decisions.

A Fundamental Life Skill

Just 20 years ago, personal finance was significantly less complex than it is today, and in many cases, parents supplemented what the schools did not teach.

We need to educate our future generations to make smarter financial decisions.

Fast forward to present day, and we now have hundreds of different home mortgage options and the burden of retirement planning is shifting from the government and traditional company pension plans to consumers through investment vehicles such as IRAs [individual retirement accounts] and 401(k)s.

Because of their own financial woes, in many cases, parents are no longer comfortable with talking to their children about the touchy subject of money and personal finance.

Sadly, research shows that financial illiteracy has reached epidemic levels with no end in sight.

Much has been done to bring awareness to other growing crises such as childhood obesity, the need to wear sunscreen, and the dangers of drug and alcohol abuse, but why has something as important as financial literacy been largely ignored?

Results from my recent online consumer survey, FinancialLiteracyQuiz.com, show that:

- Only 50 percent of those who took the survey know that property taxes and mortgage interest are tax deductible

- Only 40 percent know that their liability for credit-card fraud is limited to $50.

- Only 33 percent know what "annual percentage rate" (APR) means.

- Only 32 percent know what required deductions are taken from their paycheck.

So, why should Americans care? These are basic pieces of information that are critical to financial decisions. And the better job we do of financially educating the next generation, the more financially independent they will be. This will not only mean breaking free from ongoing support from parents or destructive financial habits, but it could potentially save a lot of money.

Our school system has an obligation to prepare students for success in a fast paced global economy. Personal finance is a subject that will affect all consumers for the rest of their lives, regardless of age, education level, or income.

Financial literacy is a fundamental life skill that needs to be properly taught in the school system, alongside traditional math, English, and science.

The public needs to put pressure on lawmakers to mandate this. Parents and students need to be vocal locally.

In the meantime, consumers need to accept personal responsibility and invest in themselves to get financially educated. They can start by reading a book, attending a seminar, or getting coaching from a trusted adviser. But they have to start now. The future of our financial lives depends on it.

8

Confessions of a Credit-Card Pusher

Jessica Silver-Greenberg

Jessica Silver-Greenberg is a reporter for BusinessWeek.com.

Credit card companies claim to have pulled back from marketing to college students, but their tactics may bypass restrictions, worrying lawmakers, university administrators, and consumer advocates. Some companies recruit college students to act as credit-card pushers, who offer T-shirts and other freebies to entice dorm residents and friends to fill out applications. Others position marketing operations near campuses, often just off school grounds. While companies claim to educate applicants about credit card usage and allege that college students' financial savvy is underestimated, new cardholders are neither advised on the cards' terms nor how to use them responsibly.

It all started as a way to make some quick cash. In 2002, at the beginning of his freshman year at the University of Pittsburgh, Ryan Rhoades needed some extra spending money. So when his friend told him about an Internet ad offering Pitt students a way to make some cash in a couple of hours, he didn't hesitate. Rhoades rounded up some of his buddies and headed over to the designated classroom at the student union.

What he saw in that room offers a view of how creative credit-card companies have become in marketing their services to college students.

An enthusiastic man who identified himself as a representative of Citibank (C) welcomed them and said they had the opportunity to make some money by signing up their fellow students for credit cards. The bounty for each completed application would be $5 to $10, depending on the kind of card. In retrospect, Rhoades feels like he and his fellow students were being recruited to become credit-card pushers. "That's exactly what it was," he says.

Salesmen at the Gates

Rhoades took the job and signed up roughly 30 students for cards. He regrets any trouble he caused other students from his actions. Still, his actions may have been most damaging to himself. He ended up with $13,000 worth of debt that he is now struggling to repay. "I hadn't learned anything about credit cards in high school, and I didn't know anything about them at the time," says Rhoades. "I was duped."

Politicians and college administrators are growing increasingly concerned about the damage that credit-card debt is causing students, and they're trying to crack down on some of the card companies' practices. They're limiting marketing on some campuses and trying to restrict the size of credit lines extended to students. Earlier this year, the state legislatures in Texas, Oklahoma, and New York moved to clamp down on credit-card marketing to college students [see BusinessWeek-.com, 9/4/07, "Majoring in Credit-Card Debt"].

As the restrictions grow, however, so too do the creative tactics marketers use to circumvent these efforts. At Columbia University in New York City, the school banned credit-card solicitations on campus. But a spokesman says the prohibition may not be that effective because the card companies set up "right outside the gates" to the school grounds. At the University of Michigan and nine other schools, JPMorgan Chase (JPM) contracted with New York-based BicyTaxi to offer students free bike-taxi rides around town. Once inside the vehicles, students are greeted with a piped-in recording promoting Chase's student credit-card program, Chase+1.

"Under Attack"

As for the University of Pittsburgh, the school had barred marketers from dormitories by 2002. But Rhoades, unaware of the restriction, marched right through the dorms to sign up his fellow students. He says he did so on his own, without discussing it with Citibank's representative. A Pittsburgh spokesman declined to comment for this story.

Politicians and college administrators are growing increasingly concerned about the damage that credit-card debt is causing students, and they're trying to crack down on some of the card companies' practices.

A spokesperson for Citibank says the company has voluntarily pulled back from marketing on college campuses. She would not specify which year the company made the decision, but says it no longer allows employees or any company it contracts with to solicit students on school grounds. "Citi does not conduct direct sales marketing on college campuses," she wrote in an e-mail. Citibank also says that it has strict guidelines for third-party vendors and that it would never condone violations of school policies.

That doesn't mean that Citibank doesn't market to college kids. The company has a specially designated card for students. And it actively markets its services near college campuses. Edward Solomon is chief executive of Campus Dimensions, which contracts with banks to market credit cards to college students. He says his company plans to visit 1,000 schools this fall to promote cards for Citibank and U.S. Bank (USB). In both cases, his company will work to steer clear of school grounds but stay close enough to attract students. "It's mostly about positioning yourself in a high traffic area," he says.

Such moves have consumer advocates up in arms. They argue that the growing problems that college students are having with credit cards need to be addressed more aggressively. If banks such as Citibank are still marketing to youngsters despite the existing restrictions, then schools and politicians need to take tougher steps. "Students are constantly under attack," says Linda Sherry, director of national priorities for Consumer Action, a San Francisco consumer education and advocacy group. "Despite colleges' best intentions, the companies just set up shop across the street."

Easy Money

Back in 2002, when Rhoades entered Pitt's student center during his freshman year, the first thing he noticed was the abundance of giveaways handed out with the credit cards. Among other things, there were about 20 boxes of T-shirts with "college" emblazoned in capital letters on the front, and a Citibank logo printed quietly under the collar. "You know I recently saw someone wearing that shirt when I was in Vermont, and I thought, damn, maybe that's another person who got a credit card because they wanted a free T-shirt," says Rhoades. "It made me mad."

Roughly 25 students were milling around the student center, discussing what their mysterious sales task would be, when the man who identified himself as a Citibank rep entered. "He told us that this was easy money to make and that all we had to do was get students to fill out applications for Citibank credit cards," recalls Rhoades.

After arming the students with a bundle of T-shirts and credit-card applications, the Citibank representative, according to Rhoades, told the group how to assuage any concerns a student might have. "He told us phrases to tell students if they were skeptical about filling out an application," says Rhoades. "He told us to say things like, 'Even if you apply, you can always cut up the card,' and 'It's easy to pay off your balance once you graduate and get a great job.'"

T-shirt Temptation

Credit counselors argue these lures—the promise of a job and the prospect of just using the card during emergencies—while highly enticing for students, often don't pan out the way that marketers promise. "If the credit card is in their wallet, many students will eventually use it," says Darryl Dahlheimer, program manager at LSS Financial Counseling Service located on the University of Minnesota campus. "I bet none of the students I gave cards to ever cut up the cards," Rhoades says. "That's what you tell yourself, but it's too tempting."

Campus Dimensions' Solomon believes students are much more informed and savvy than critics suggest. With every credit-card application, Solomon tries to educate students about the various elements of the card, explaining interest rates, balance transfers, and responsible credit usage. "We try to give students good information from a marketing standpoint, as well as realistic information," he says.

Rhoades had no time to teach his fellow students about the pros and cons of credit. In fact, he wouldn't have known what to say if they had asked. All he wanted to do was sign up students. Without prompting from the Citibank representative, he went into one of the dorms, started on the third floor, and solicited on every floor until he reached the 20th. He was pretty successful, signing up roughly 29 students in a single morning. "Most of the students just wanted the T-shirt, and so I told them to fill out the application anyway," remembers Rhoades. "I just told them to fill it out and never use the card again."

Warning Needed

Rhoades remembers that even though the credit-card application terms and conditions were listed in fine print, none of the students even glanced at them. His observation echoes a common criticism that students aren't educated about what they are signing when getting a credit card. "Students are rarely given financial literacy training," notes Dahlheimer. "And access to cards in the absence of a warning is like giving car keys to someone who has never been taught to drive." Rhoades recalls that the whole process was so fast that students had little time to glance at the application. "We were in a hurry to get people to sign up and they just did it, as a favor or because they didn't care," he says.

At the end of the morning, exhausted from traipsing around campus, Rhoades surveyed his progress. He was just one application short of getting a cash bonus so he decided to fill one out himself. After marketing the cards all morning, he had begun to buy his own sales pitch and since there was no commitment, he quickly filled it out.

It took just seconds. But now, five years later, he's struggling with the $13,000 of debt that he accrued across several different credit cards after using them to pay for dinners, movies, and car repairs. "They should put warnings on credit cards like they do on cigarettes," he says, "to make sure people know how dangerous the cards are."

9

Credit Card Companies Responsibly Market to College Students

Zack Martin

Zack Martin is an editor at Avisian, a consulting firm specializing in identity technology.

Under criticism for their marketing methods on college campuses, credit card issuers are trying new ways to reach out to the youth market. Instead of bombarding them with giveaways and applications, some insightful companies court college students with meaningful opportunities. For example, to appeal to their academic and career aspirations, MasterCard has sponsored once-in-a-lifetime sports and music internships for contestants who wrote winning essays. These endeavors not only create favorable brand awareness within the youth market, but also enrich college students' lives and communities.

With a swing of the bat Texas Ranger Hank Blaylock gave home-field advantage to the American League for the 2003 World Series, catapulting the team to a 7-6 win in the 74th Annual All-Star Game.

And while the event will be remembered by many, for 12 college students some of the excitement came before the game's first pitch.

The vast majority of the assembled 47,609 baseball fans in attendance at Chicago's U.S. Cellular Field didn't know what to make of the dozen 20-somethings near home plate, clad in dark blue golf shirts with an orange and yellow circle insignia on them. Then, over the public-address system, it was announced that the students were winners of MasterCard International's Priceless Edge program, which allows college students between ages 18 and 25 the opportunity to gain real-world experience in the sports industry.

Different Ways to Hit the Youth Market

Oftentimes credit card issuers are maligned for their marketing methods on college campuses, offering students a free water bottle or other giveaway and then issuing cards that enable students to pile up debt that takes years to pay off. The average college student carries $3,000 in card debt upon graduation, according to Newton, Mass.-based American Consumer Credit Counseling.

Under such criticism, card marketers recently have tried to find different ways to hit the youth market, especially college students, in a responsible way. The youth market, ages 13 to 24, represents 20% of the population and is growing faster than the overall population, according to research from Price WaterhouseCoopers. The age group spends $260 billion a year and has influence over another $600 billion in spending.

MasterCard is attempting to hit the higher tier of that youth demographic by focusing on 18- to 25-year-olds with its Priceless Edge campaign. The campaign includes student-oriented print advertising, broadcast commercials, and on-campus signs. The decision to offer the age group an internship came through the association's research showing students are very concerned about careers, says Elisa Romm, vice president of brand building at MasterCard.

Launched in 2002, the program originally offered students the opportunity to intern with a record company. Some 12,000 students submitted essays last year [in 2002], with 50 selected for a five-week course and 12 receiving internships to help produce a music documentary.

MasterCard expanded the program this year to include a sports internship as well as music. The association told students about the program through campus advertising and related marketing, and national television ads. MasterCard wouldn't disclose the cost of the program.

Some 32,000 students submitted essays to be eligible for this year's program, which took 100 semifinalists to Vanderbilt University in Nashville, Tenn., for a five-week course on either the sports or the music business. After the five weeks, the winners from the sports and music programs were placed in internships, mostly to learn about marketing. The 12 sports students interned for either the St. Louis Cardinals or New York Mets. The 12 music students went to the Santa Monica, Calif., offices of Interscope Geffen A&M records.

Prior to heading out to those locations, all 24 interns were in Chicago to receive some hands-on experience in their respective fields. The music interns helped set up for the Lollapalooza music festival in July.

Those from the sports side worked various activities connected with the All-Star Game, including escorting team mascots around the ballpark and working the All-Star Fan Fest, before moving on to their teams.

"It was kind of like being in Disneyland," says Peter Forsberg, one of the sports interns who attends Princeton University.

The interns also worked with Hall of Fame slugger George Brett, a MasterCard spokesperson during the midsummer classic. Brett serves as special adviser to the Kansas City Royals, his former team, and also has ownership stakes in a number of sports organizations, including minor league baseball teams. Brett spoke to the students about the importance of having real-world experience in the sports industry and gave Andy Mielnik, one of the interns, an unforgettable experience.

Mielnik, attending Baylor University, was standing on the field when Brett walked up to him and took him to meet a friend. At first Mielnik thought he was going to meet a reporter or another intern, but Brett introduced him to St. Louis Cardinal outfielder Albert Pujols "I was speechless," he says.

Investment in Community

While the opportunity to meet Major League Baseball players is one none of these 12 sports students will forget, some industry observers question whether a small-scale internship program is an effective way to reach the youth market. Scott Strumello, an analyst with Westbury, N.Y.-based Auriemma Consulting Group Inc., says it's tough to see this as youth marketing.

"I would call it philanthropy, it's an investment into the community," he says. "It's not clear to me how this is reaching out to youth markets." Auriemma performs market research in the credit card industry.

There is more of a focus on educating students, rather than just giving them a card and letting them charge away.

The program, however, could give an overall boost to MasterCard's brand over time, according to Strumello.

"They're getting the name in front of those consumers," he says.

Anything that can be done to "put a positive face on credit cards" is good, according to Ed Solomon, president of Philadelphia-based College Credit Card Corp., which has marketed cards to college students since the 1970s and recently did work for Discover and Citibank.

Marketing credit cards to college students has changed in the past few years, Solomon says. There is more of a focus on educating students, rather than just giving them a card and letting them charge away.

Marketers also have to be aware that this age demographic doesn't like to be hit over the head with advertising, says Tony Sgro, president of EdVenture Partners, an Orinda, Calif.-based youth-marketing firm.

"Most research says Generation Y doesn't want to be marketed in your face," he says. "They're highly mistrustful and can tell good advertising from bad."

Sgro says lifestyle-based marketing, like Priceless Edge, is the correct way to hit the youth market now. EdVenture Partners teams with universities around the country to offer students real-world experience in various fields. The firm has worked with Citibank to have students run marketing campaigns on credit awareness.

Not surprisingly, the students involved in Priceless Edge have a positive view of MasterCard now, whereas before they might not have given the brand much thought.

"MasterCard, Discover, and Visa bombard you with applications," says Adam Lobel of St. Louis. "But now going through this has developed a whole new brand loyalty for me to MasterCard."

Jennifer Dutko, from Oregon State University, doesn't have a credit card.

"I always thought of them as signing up for this and get a free towel," she says. But now she will be applying for a MasterCard.

10

Credit Card Marketing Efforts to College Students Should Be Regulated

Erica L. Williams

Erica L. Williams is policy and advocacy manager of Campus Progress Action, a part of the policy think tank Center for American Progress.

The predatory practices used by the credit card industry to market to college students must be regulated. With giveaways and incentives, companies lure students—on and off campus, at sporting events, around dorms—into applying for cards with high interest rates, multiple fees, and complex terms. As a result, thousands of young adults accumulate looming credit card debt before graduating, often using cards to pay for academic fees, textbooks, and even tuition. To address this crisis, college students should continue to protest against credit card companies marketing on campus, and they should advocate for increased personal information privacy. Congress also should ban the most abusive and unfair credit card practices and improve the disclosure of terms, billing statements, and payments to cardholders.

Erica L. Williams, "Testimony of Campus Progress Action Before U.S. House Subcommittee on Financial Institutions and Consumer Credit On Problems Credit Card Practices Affecting Students," *www.americanprogress.org*, July 26, 2008. Copyright © 2008 Center for American Progress. Reproduced by permission.

Testimony of Campus Progress Action Before U.S. House Subcommittee on Financial Institutions and Consumer Credit on Problems Credit Card Practices Affecting Students, June 26, 2008

Chairwoman Maloney, Ranking Member Biggert, and members of the committee:

I am Erica L. Williams, Policy and Advocacy Manager of Campus Progress Action. Campus Progress Action is part of the Center for American Progress Action Fund. Along with our sister organization, Campus Progress, which is part of the Center for American Progress, we work to help young people make their voices heard on issues that matter. Through grassroots issue campaigns, public events, an online magazine, a blog, and student publications, we act to empower new progressive leaders nationwide as they develop fresh ideas, communicate in new ways, and build a strong progressive movement.

First, let me thank you for the opportunity to testify on behalf of the young people on over 500 campuses and communities with whom we work.

The issue of credit card debt is one that impacts many Americans, and much already has been presented to the committee about the important role that Congress should and must play in mandating fair credit card practices.

My testimony this afternoon will not only reinforce that point, but will also seek to convince you of two things: First, that young people, especially students, are uniquely impacted by credit card debt and the abusive practices of credit card companies. Second, that this negative impact can only be made better through an approach with legislative action at its center.

Two years ago, Campus Progress began engaging students around the country in a discussion about debt in higher education through our Debt Hits Hard campaign. The campaign focused primarily on rising college costs and student loans.

But as we began that work, something else became increasingly evident. We realized that credit card debt and the process through which it is incurred is an equally important part of understanding the financial lives and burdens of young people.

Since so many student credit cards have high annual percentage rates . . . the longer these students wait to pay the cards off, the more money they'll pay in the form of interest.

If there is one common experience that college students share, it is the experience of living in debt. Compared to previous generations, today's young adults have not only been forced to borrow for their education but also for their expenses while in college.

According to Nellie Mae, the average undergraduate has $2,200 in credit card debt. That figure jumps to $5,800 for graduate students. Since so many student credit cards have high annual percentage rates, often at higher rates than the rest of the population given their thinner credit files, the longer these students wait to pay the cards off, the more money they'll pay in the form of interest.[1]

As organizations like Center for American Progress, U.S. PIRG and Demos began producing the evidence of this growing and unique student problem through reports, statistics, and solid research, Campus Progress Action continued to do what we do best: talk with students and give them the tools to make their voices heard about the issues that affect them the

---

1. Nellie Mae, "Undergraduate Students and Credit Cards in 2004: An Analysis of Usage Rates and Trends," 2005, available at http://www.nelliemae.com/pdf/ccstudy_2005.pdf.

most. And they spoke out about predatory credit card practices and the overwhelming weight of that debt loudly and clearly.

Through a series of public forums around the country, from Broward Community College in Fort Lauderdale, Florida to Purdue University in Indiana, we brought together students and experts to discuss the growing problem of credit card debt on college campuses. At each event we heard the same: Banks and lenders are profiting off of young people's financial inexperience, partnerships and relationships with universities, and strategic and deliberate targeting.

As a young professional myself, not yet 5 years out of college, I can trace my relationship with credit card debt back to my freshman year. I had been warned by my mother about credit cards and tried to stayed away from them at all cost. Mail solicitations jammed my tiny dorm mailbox and fliers on bulletin boards greeted me every day as I walked out of the building. Because of my lack of faith in the integrity of the credit card industry and a feeling of vulnerability, I had a fear of credit cards that fortunately kept me away from accumulating an exorbitant amount of debt. But there were indeed nights when, after my meal plan was overextended, the burden of student debt was so great and the money from my work-study job so low, that I desperately wanted and needed to use a credit card for meals and social activities.

For every story like mine, there are thousands of stories like that of Kali Dun, a student from the University of Virginia. Now a young professional with over $7,000 in credit card debt, she shared with Campus Progress her experience with credit cards in college. When asked about the presence of companies on campus she said, "They were everywhere . . . like vultures. Outside of my dorm, at football games, and in the quad. I took their teddy bears, free pizza, tote bags, and complicated, convoluted sign up forms." By her junior year, Kali had opened three credit cards, all on campus, and had incurred nearly $3,000 in debt. Along with the giveaways and incentives, she took also too high fees, heavy interest rate burdens, and complex terms, three credit card practices that have been proven to heighten the risk of default. And default she did. As a senior, Kali graduated with over $5,000 in credit card debt.

Kali's story is but one of many that we continue to hear from students. It illustrates the key challenges that college students face with regard to credit cards:

1. Aggressive marketing and targeting by credit card companies.

With regard to marketing, companies use a variety of aggressive techniques, from buying lists from schools and entering into exclusive marketing arrangements with schools to marketing directly to students through the mail, over the phone, on bulletin boards and through aggressive on-campus and near-campus tabling—facilitated by so-called "free gifts."[2]

2. High fees, heavy interest rates, and complex terms.

The credit card debt that students incur from these credit experiences tends to carry substantially higher costs than other forms of credit due to myriad fees in addition to high interest rates. The result is that many students unwittingly slide deeper and deeper into debt as they fall prey to the lack of transparency in credit cards.

But credit card companies are notorious for aggressive marketing and fine print. Why is this situation particularly damaging for students?

Here is a snapshot of college-age young people at 18–24 years of age:

- According to a 2004 study by Nellie Mae, 76 percent of undergrads have credit cards, and the average under-

2. Tamara Draut and Javier Silva, "Generation Broke: The Growth of Debt Among Young Americans," Demos, 2004, p. 7.

graduate has $2,200 in credit card debt. Additionally, they will amass, on average, almost $20,000 in student debt.[3]

- Another study found that 18- to 24-year-olds in 1989 devoted 13 percent of their income to debt payments. Today's 18- to 24-year-olds devote 22 percent of their income to servicing their debt.

- One-fourth of the students surveyed in US PIRG's 2008 Campus Credit Card Trap report said that they have paid a late fee, and 15 percent have paid an "over the limit" fee. Credit card companies will often impose a "penalty rate" of 30 percent or more after just one or two late payments, and this interest rate will often last for six months or more. Sometimes, customers are charged a penalty rate because they were late on a different loan (this is called "risk-based re-pricing" or "universal default"), and some banks manipulate the due dates from one month to another to rack up late fees.[4]

Credit cards are increasingly being used for academic fees and textbooks.

Major borrowing from credit card companies is like visiting a Las Vegas casino—it's a gamble and the odds are against you. But as college students, the analogy goes a step further. Imagine that you entered the casino every time you walked out of class, or out of the cafeteria. Or if fliers for the casino were taped on the walls of every bathroom, and blackjack dealers were calling your dorm room with promises of free

3. Nellie Mae, "Undergraduate Students and Credit Cards in 2004: An Analysis of Usage Rates and Trends."
4. U.S. PIRG, "Campus Credit Card Trap," available at http://www.truthaboutcredit.org/campus-credit-card-trap.

casino chips—all during the most important time in your financial life. The casino wants college students, and needing the money, they don't realize that this gamble is one that has implications for the next 5, 10, or 20 years.

To be clear, this accumulated credit card debt is not always the result of irresponsible spending and late night pizza runs—it is also the result of academic fees and textbooks. U.S. PIRG's research has shown[5] that some students use their credit cards to pay for their core tuition. Credit cards are increasingly being used for academic fees and textbooks. In exchange for using this form of payment for academic needs, students are rewarded with high interest rates, high debt-to-credit ratios, low credit scores, and blemishes in the infancy of their credit history that will haunt them for years. Young people who become delinquent on credit cards due to the lack of transparency can damage their credit score and run the risk of paying a higher rate on their car loans, home loans, and other loans in the future.

Not only are college students and other young people in perhaps the most vital and vulnerable point of their financial lives, their future economic health often depends on decisions made during this period. Students saddled with credit card debt upon graduation can pay up to 25 cents of every dollar they earn servicing their debt: their credit cards, student loans, and other loans.[6] To add to this, today's young adults are joining the job market during a time when incomes have been stagnant and when costs for health care and retirement benefits are increasingly being shifted from employers to employees. Recent graduates also find that the job market is changing rapidly, so much so that the career paths that their education prepared them for may soon disappear. This generation—which is the future middle class of workers—can ill afford to

5. Ibid.
6. Tamara Draut, *Strapped: Why America's 20- and 30-Somethings Can't Get Ahead* (New York: Doubleday, 2006).

be financially compromised. These and other factors paint the following harrowing picture of life after college:

- A 2006 poll of 3 million twentysomethings from *USA Today* and Experian, the credit-reporting agency, found that nearly half of twentysomethings have stopped paying a debt, forcing lenders to "charge off" the debt and sell it to a collection agency, or had cars repossessed or sought bankruptcy protection.[7]

- A poll of twentysomethings by *USA TODAY* and the National Endowment for Financial Education found that 60 percent feel they're facing tougher financial pressures than young people did in previous generations. And 30 percent say they worry frequently about their debt.[8]

- The Boomerang Effect, young adults returning to live with their parents, is quickly growing. The 2000 Census found that more than 25 percent of 18- to 34-year-olds had moved back in with family at the time the Census was taken. In 2006, Experience Inc., which provides career services to link college grads with jobs, found that 58 percent of the twentysomethings it surveyed had moved back home after college. Of those, 32 percent stayed for more than a year, according to its survey of 320.[9]

- Debt has forced some young people to change their career plans. Of those surveyed in the 2006 *USA Today/* NEFE poll, 22 percent say they've taken a job they otherwise wouldn't have because they needed more money

---

7. Mindy Fetterman and Barbara Hansen, "Young people struggle to deal with kiss of debt," *USA TODAY*, November 19, 2006, available at http://www.usatoday.com/money/perfi/credit/2006-11-19-young-and-in-debtcover_ x.htm.
8. Ibid.
9. Ibid.

to pay off student-loan debt. Twenty-nine percent say they've put off or chosen not to pursue more education because they have so much debt already. And 26 percent have put off buying a home for the same reason.[10]

- Average credit card debt among indebted young adults increased by 55 percent between 1992 and 2001, to $4,088.[11]

- The average credit card indebted young adult household now spends nearly 24 percent of its income on debt payments, four percentage points more, on average, than young adults did in 1992.[12]

- Among young adult households with incomes below $50,000 (two-thirds of young households), nearly one in five with credit card debt is in debt hardship— spending over 40 percent of their income servicing debt, including mortgages and student loans.[13]

- Young Americans now have the second highest rate of bankruptcy, just after those aged 35 to 44. The rate among 25 to 34-year-olds increased between 1991 and 2001, indicating that this generation is more likely to file bankruptcy as young adults than were young Boomers at the same age.[14]

College students are in trouble, and credit card companies are partly to blame.

As a result of over-the-top credit card marketing on campuses, terrible credit card terms and conditions, and an economy that no longer provides as many well-paying jobs

10. Ibid.
11. Draut and Silva, "Generation Broke: The Growth of Debt Among Young Americans."
12. Ibid.
13. Ibid.
14. Ibid.

with good benefits as it once did, young adults, post-college, are facing overwhelming odds to achieve financial health, in large part as a result of the credit card debt from their undergraduate years. We are, as Anya Kamenetz's book of the same name labeled us, Generation Debt. Significant, unmanageable credit debt and a cycle of post-graduation payments, default, and potential bankruptcy, impacts our families (due to limited options for living arrangements and delayed marriage rates) and our communities (due to job decisions made strictly with debt payments in mind).

So we now know the scope of the problem. College students are in trouble, and credit card companies are partly to blame. But what about the solution?

First, students will continue their campaigns on the state and campus level to not allow credit card marketing on campus, to keep colleges and universities from sharing students and alumni lists to credit card marketers, and to improve financial literacy among young adults.

But Congress also has its role to play. We submit two policy ideas. First, we urge Congress to take the extra step and, with young people in mind, *mandate a higher level of fairness in credit card terms and conditions by banning several of the most abusive credit card practices.* Currently, young people who want to use credit cards responsibly have a difficult time determining their terms and conditions, and have difficulty cost-shopping among different credit cards. And further, those who endeavor to read their voluminous cardholder agreements often find a clause to the effect of: "We reserve the right to change the terms at any time for any reason." Congress should mandate that card issuers give cardholders at least 45 days notice of any interest rate increases and the right to cancel their card and pay off the existing balance before the increase takes place.

Second, the Federal Reserve's proposed changes to Regulation Z would go a long way to improve the effectiveness of the marketing disclosures, account opening statements, and billing statements that young adults receive. This would ensure that information is provided in a timely manner and in a form that is readily understandable. Congress could go a step further by enacting more creative ways of disclosing the most important information. This can be done by requiring disclosure of the length of time it will take to pay off an account if only the minimum payment is made. In this way, students could better gauge the long-term costs of putting debt on their credit cards.

Legislative action to protect against abuses by credit card companies is a fundamental issue of fairness and protection of America's future—young Americans—when they are arguably in the most vulnerable and important phase of their financial lives.

11

Credit Card Marketing Efforts to College Students Should Not Be Regulated

Kenneth J. Clayton

Kenneth J. Clayton is senior vice president and general counsel of the American Bankers Association's (ABA) Card Policy Council.

Not everyone will use credit cards responsibly, and managing large debts can be stressful. However, stories of college students racking up debt do not reflect the reality of how this age group uses credit cards. On the contrary, most students carry lower debts and use cards more responsibly than does the general population. And with lower limits and fees, student credit cards offer the security and flexibility to cover unexpected expenses, medical emergencies, and the costs of books and tuition. Moreover, the majority of young cardholders obtain credit cards through their banks, not from on-campus display tables. In the end, regulating the marketing practices of credit card companies would restrict college students from having access to the usefulness of credit cards.

Chairwoman [Carolyn] Maloney and members of the Subcommittee, my name is Kenneth J. Clayton, senior vice president and general counsel of the American Bankers Association (ABA) Card Policy Council, the group within the ABA

Kenneth J. Clayton, "Testimony of Kenneth J. Clayton on Behalf of the American Bankers Association Before the Subcommittee on Financial Institutions and Consumer Credit, Committee on Financial Services, United States House of Representatives," in *financialservices.house.gov*, June 26, 2008.

that deals with card issues. ABA works to enhance the competitiveness of the nation's banking industry and strengthen America's economy and communities. Its members—the majority of which are banks with less than $125 million in assets—represent over 95 percent of the industry's $13.3 trillion in assets and employ over 2 million men and women.

We appreciate, Madame Chairwoman, the opportunity to appear today to discuss college students' rights as adults to obtain and use credit cards. We certainly acknowledge at the outset that not all students will manage debt in a responsible way, just as not all adults in general will manage debt without experiencing problems. Dealing with debt problems at any age can be very stressful and our card companies do their best to deal with each individual situation quickly to help resolve the problem. However, anecdotes of student problems in the card area fail to paint the real picture that students, as a broader group, are in fact managing their credit obligations well. Importantly, we fear that policy decisions made on the basis of anecdotes will end up hurting the vast majority of young adults who have shown they are capable of managing their finances responsibly. As such, they will be denied the full benefits of a very valuable payment and credit instrument.

It is also important to note that despite their relative inexperience, *college-age individuals are adults*. They have the right to contract, work, marry, serve in the armed forces, and vote. They have the right—and responsibility—to exercise independent judgment in these areas, aided by the educational tools that we in society can provide. We hope policymakers will be mindful to not create artificial barriers to the exercise of these independent choices, recognizing that in creating such barriers, you may be limiting the significant benefits that credit products have to offer for the vast majority of young adults.

In my statement today, I would like to focus on four major themes:

- Credit cards provide an invaluable service to students;

- Students have shown they use credit responsibly;

- Barriers to access will impose hardships on the vast majority of students who have demonstrated they can manage credit card use responsibly; and

- Financial education for young adults is critical to financial success.

Credit Cards Provide an Invaluable Service to Students

Credit cards have become an integral, convenient and important part of student life. They are an instant means of payment for purchases; they are safer than cash, accepted more places than checks, and can be used almost anywhere. They provide a flexible and convenient way for students to buy books and other essentials, as well as purchase airline tickets or rent cars. The Government Accountability Office (GAO) in the most recent, comprehensive government study undertaken on student card use found that some 77 percent of students used their cards for routine personal expenses, 57 percent for books and supplies, and 12 percent to pay tuition and fees (though over half of the last category paid their charges in full right away). Clearly, cards have become an invaluable tool for students' everyday needs.

Moreover, credit cards provide a particularly important safety net for emergencies. In that same GAO study, researchers found that 67 percent of students reported that they used their credit cards for occasional and emergency expenses, illustrating the importance of having access to such cards for unexpected circumstances. "Credit cards provided convenience and security and were especially useful in emergencies, allowing students to pay for unplanned medical expenses or purchase airplane tickets home."

For many consumers, and particularly for students, credit cards are also the point of entry into the world of credit.

Credit card use establishes credit histories, which help people to obtain jobs, rent and buy homes, or purchase cars and other big-ticket items. In fact, according to a 2008 study by Student Monitor, 53 percent of college students of who obtained a credit card did so to establish a credit history. Credit histories permit individuals to demonstrate their creditworthiness, and therefore have dramatically expanded access to credit to all members of society in the most efficient, non-discriminatory way possible.

A Student Monitor survey indicated that only 2 percent of students obtained their cards by filling out an application at a display on campus.

Banks recognize that applying for a credit card may be a college student's first independent experience with the bank and want it to be the start of a positive, life-long customer relationship. As such, banks have a vested interest in responsible underwriting, so as to ensure ongoing customer satisfaction. They establish low credit limits and lower fees, they constantly monitor student accounts, and have instituted significant financial literacy programs. Students also receive a wide range of disclosures on the terms of agreement both in the account-opening procedures and on an ongoing basis. All of these efforts are focused on creating a successful relationship with young adults new to this financial tool.

Banks are also cautious about marketing efforts, generally focusing on depository accounts rather than credit accounts. In fact, checking accounts are typically the lead product for marketing efforts to students, and credit cards are offered as a supplement to this. As a result, the vast majority of credit cards obtained by students come from students visiting the bank branch to begin a broader account relationship. Recent information from one member bank suggests 65 percent of student credit card accounts were opened through banking centers, allowing for important education on financial literacy as a part of interaction with bank staff. The remaining card accounts are opened by students over the Internet, in response to direct mail solicitations, or through telemarketing initiatives. A Student Monitor survey indicated that only 2 percent of students obtained their cards by filling out an application at a display on campus. This reflects the reality that student card accounts are opened through various distribution channels, many of which are not targeted to students at all but members of the general population that share a common characteristic, (e.g., those that open checking accounts or other accounts within the institution). This is not to say that various institutions are not interested in the student market, just that criticism directed at specific marketing techniques tends to overstate the real world experience.

---

74 percent of monthly college spending is with cash and debit cards. Only 7 percent is with credit cards.

Students Have Shown They Use Credit Responsibly

It is perhaps because of banks' focus on a lasting relationship that students have shown that they can use credit more responsibly than the general population. Recent studies have found that student accounts generally have lower balances and lower credit limits, and that students use them less than the general population. And although seventy percent of undergraduates and post-graduates have outstanding debt, the bulk of this debt is from student loans.

Consider the following statistics:

- 41 percent of college students have a credit card.

- Of the students with cards, about 65 percent pay their bills in full every month, which is *higher than the general adult population.*

- Among the 35 percent that do not pay their balances in full every month, the average balance is $452. This is down 19 percent from 2007. Moreover, this balance is approximately one-third the size of the average balance for active non-student young adult accounts and one-fourth the size of active accounts for older adults.

- 74 percent of monthly college spending is with cash and debit cards. Only 7 percent is with credit cards.

Certainly, there are examples of students who took on more debt than they were ultimately able to manage. But in the vast majority of cases, students are acting responsibly and meeting their obligations. This fact is borne out when examining portfolios of student credit card accounts at banks. These portfolios are considered low-risk, and their performance is better than the general population.

Barriers to Access Will Impose Hardships on Students Who Manage Credit Card Use Responsibly

As previously noted, credit cards provide a flexible and convenient way to manage student spending. Students buy books and other student essentials, purchase airline tickets, rent cars and pay for medical and other emergencies with their credit cards. Thus, credit cards represent an important tool for managing both day-to-day needs and unexpected events. Restricting access to this form of credit would result in great financial hardship for most college students *and their families*.

Notwithstanding that fact, Congress and several state legislatures have introduced legislation that would have the effect of limiting or preventing categories of college students from obtaining a credit card. Some proposals have taken the form of arbitrary limits on available credit. Others have limited the amount of credit available on a single card, or would limit the amount of cards a student may have. Still others would impose liability on lenders who, with the benefit of hindsight, did not make correct judgments regarding the creditworthiness of a student borrower. Such barriers to credit access can create real hardships for students, the vast majority of which have demonstrated their ability to manage their credit cards responsibly.

It is also important to remember that "college students" are hardly a homogenous group. A popular misconception is that the typical college student lives on campus and attends a four-year institution. The fact is that *only 16 percent of students are full-time undergraduates residing on campus*—fewer than three million of the more than 17 million students enrolled today. Today's students don't fit the traditional mold: 40 percent study part-time, 40 percent attend two-year institutions, 40 percent are older than 25, and 58 percent are older than 22. While going to school, these "non-traditional" adult college students often work full or part time and many have families. Thus, efforts to regulate access to credit may impose different hardships on different categories of "students" based on their life situations, and will clearly result in consequences unanticipated to policymakers.

These examples show the difficulty in imposing artificial restraints on the dissemination of credit to a particular category of adult borrower. They also reflect a failure to acknowledge that the vast majority of adult students handle their credit responsibly, making such restrictions unnecessary.

Financial Education for Young Adults Is Critical to Financial Success

As has often been noted, the key to responsible card use lies in improvements in financial literacy. Financial education is the key that allows students of all types to unlock their financial future and use many financial tools wisely—credit being just one of these tools. Understanding financial matters is a critical part of success in life, and this work begins in the home and in early school experiences.

Most banks that issue credit cards are engaged in a wide variety of financial literacy and school education efforts, often in partnership with consumer groups, and many of these programs include training for young people using credit for the first time. The U.S. Department of the Treasury is also actively engaged in a nationwide, coordinated effort on financial literacy through the National Literacy and Education Commission. That Commission, created by Congress in 2003 as part of the "Financial Literacy and Education Improvement Act" (Title V of the Fair and Accurate Credit Transactions Act of 2003 [FACT Act]), among other things, encourages government and private sector efforts to promote financial literacy as well as develop a national strategy on the subject. Significant Congressional efforts to promote financial literacy have also been undertaken, the most recent example involving the efforts by the Financial and Economic Literacy Caucus, co-chaired by Representatives Ruben Hinojosa (D-TX) and Subcommittee Ranking Member Judy Biggert (R-IL). In addition, the ABA has also been involved in various financial literacy efforts through our ABA Education Foundation, which sponsors the annual "Get Smart About Credit Day" in October to educate young adults about the proper use of credit. ABA has catalogued many of the efforts of our member institutions to provide financial education to consumers.

The answer then is to train students—and all adults—in the responsible management of credit and, indeed, the wise use of all financial tools. Banks, schools, and policy-makers have been working to accomplish this goal, while at the same time enabling adults to access the products they need in order to carry out daily activities, manage surprise expenses, and establish a credit history that will allow them to purchase an automobile or a home when they graduate. Credit cards are one product that enables students to do this, even though the amount of debt students carry on cards is small compared to their total debt load. Restricting access to this form of credit would result in great financial hardship for most card-holding college students and their families.

12

Rising Credit Card Interest Rates Hurt Students

Matthew Palevsky and Thibault Chareton

Matthew Palevsky is a blogger and reporter for the Huffington Post. *Thibault Chareton is a blogger and writer.*

College students are increasingly using credit cards to finance their education. Many of these students are now becoming strapped by rising credit card interest rates of more than 29 percent in some cases, and some recent college graduates have been forced to move back in with their parents to avoid bankruptcy. Still, credit card companies continue to aggressively market to college students.

Surging credit card rates over the past few months have created a desperate situation for many college students and graduates. While the percentage of American college students and graduates in debt has remained stable in recent years, the average debt per student has risen significantly.

The College Board reports that in each year between 2000–01 and 2006–07 approximately 60 percent of bachelor degree recipients borrowed money to finance their education, but the amount borrowed rose 18 percent during the same period. The total amount of education loans—both federal and private—more than doubled from $41 billion in 1997–98 to $85 billion in 2007–08 due to inflated tuition costs and stagnant blue-collar wages.

A number of HuffPost [www.HuffingtonPost.com] readers, both students and parents, have shared their stories with us.

"This school year for me has been the worst yet," wrote Nadya Lateef, a 24-year-old senior at California State University in Long Beach. She says she had to take out several student loans and has worked part-time while taking classes full-time. Still, money has "not been anywhere near enough," she wrote. As a result, she says she must rely on her credit cards to cover even her most basic expenses.

"My credit card balances have skyrocketed. My spending is frugal yet every week I have to use my credit cards to pay for expenses. For my groceries, for my gas, for school supplies, even to pay for my own degree check report so that I can graduate," Lateef said.

A 2006 report by the American Council on Education showed that more than 12 percent of students use credit cards to pay for tuition.

Recently, Lateef says her situation became even more precarious when Citibank notified her that the interest rate on her credit card would rise to 29.99 percent. Lateef does not know how she will be able to pay her bills and she has had a hard time focusing on her studies: "The more hours I work to pay my credit card debt the more my school work suffers."

More than 12 percent of students use credit cards to pay for tuition.

Beth Leiker from Los Angeles described how her daughter, a recent graduate who put her last semester of college on her Citibank credit card, recently received a notice warning that her interest rate would rise to 29.90 percent, despite her good credit history.

"She just graduated from college in June, got a job right away but her student loans came due and now her credit card jumped the rate to a point where she can't keep up. If she didn't live with me, she'd be going bankrupt. She has friends who can't get a job or got laid off. . . . They are in dire straights, each moving back in with their parents who, like me, are also facing layoffs and financial problems." Leiker has seen her own interest rate escalate to 29.90 percent on her Capital One credit card.

Jessica Pardee, a doctoral student in sociology and a visiting instructor at the University of Central Florida, says she encountered the same problem with Capital One. "I pay my bill on time, I pay in full. I pay the interest without complaint if I carry a balance. So imagine my anger when my interest rate was increased from 8.90 percent to 17.90 percent," she wrote, denouncing what she calls an "interest pillaging" from banks and credit card companies.

Banks and credit card companies continue to saturate the ad market and make sure they remain visible on campuses around the country in an effort to solicit new accounts from students.

In March 2008, the US Public Interest Research Group [PIRG] published a survey showing that 76 percent of students had stopped at tables to look at credit card offers during school events, often lured by free gifts. The study also found that 80 percent of students have received mail from credit card companies, some more than once a month. According to PIRG, many students signed up for a credit card without fully understanding the terms of the contract.

Organizations to Contact

The editors have compiled the following list of organizations concerned with the issues debated in this book. The descriptions are derived from materials provided by the organizations. All have publications or information available for interested readers. The list was compiled on the date of publication of the present volume; the information provided here may change. Be aware that many organizations take several weeks or longer to respond to inquiries, so allow as much time as possible.

American Bankers Association (ABA)
1120 Connecticut Ave. NW, Washington, DC   20036
(800) 226-5377
Web site: www.aba.com

Founded in 1875 and based in Washington, D.C., the ABA brings together banks of all sizes and charters into one association. ABA works to enhance the competitiveness of the nation's banking industry and to strengthen America's economy and communities. Its members—the majority of which are banks with less than $125 million in assets—represent more than 95 percent of the industry's $13.6 trillion in assets and employ more than two million men and women. ABA's Get Smart About Credit program is a national financial education program that helps bankers teach students about wise credit use. Volunteer bankers teach thousands through classroom lessons, and others can use Get Smart About Credit resources from the ABA Education Foundation and individual financial institutions. The association also publishes brochures on credit and personal finance.

Campus Progress Action
1333 H St. NW, 1st Floor, Washington, DC   20005
(202) 682-1611

e-mail: campus@campusprogressaction.org
Web site: www.campusprogressaction.org

Campus Progress Action, part of the Center for American
Progress Action Fund, works to help young people—advocates, activists, journalists, artists, and others—to make their
voices heard on issues that matter. It engages in advocacy, coa-
lition, and media work on key policy issues of importance to
young people; advances grassroots issue campaigns on campuses and in communities; and trains young people in media,
policy, writing, grassroots organizing, and other critical skills.
It opposes credit card marketing on college campuses as well
as unfair consumer practices. Its Debt Hits Hard program is a
national campaign that promotes access to college and aims to
reduce student debt through strong and fair financial aid policies. Working with partners in the Campaign for College Af-
fordability, Campus Progress advocates for raising federal Pell
Grants, cutting student loan interest rates, and ending waste-
ful subsidies to lenders.

Consumer Action
221 Main St., Suite 480, San Francisco, CA   94105
(415) 777-9635
Web site: www.consumer-action.org

Consumer Action is a nonprofit, membership-based organization that was founded in San Francisco in 1971. Consumer
Action has continued to serve consumers nationwide by ad-
vancing consumer rights; referring consumers to complaint-
handling agencies through its free hotline; publishing educational materials in Chinese, English, Korean, Spanish,
Vietnamese, and other languages; advocating for consumers in
the media and before lawmakers; and comparing prices on
credit cards, bank accounts, and long distance services.

Consumer Federation of America (CFA)
1620 Eye St. NW, Suite 200, Washington, DC   20006
(202) 387-6121

e-mail: cfa@consumerfed.org
Web site: www.consumerfed.org

Since 1968, CFA has provided consumers a voice in decisions that affect their lives. CFA's professional staff gathers facts, analyzes issues, and disseminates information to the public, policy makers, and the rest of the consumer movement. The size and diversity of its membership—approximately 280 non-profit organizations from throughout the nation with a combined membership exceeding 50 million people—enables CFA to speak for virtually all consumers. In particular, CFA looks out for those who have the greatest needs, especially the least affluent. The organization's Web site publishes brochures, studies, fact sheets, and transcripts of testimony on a wide variety of consumer topics, including credit.

Consumer Watchdog

1750 Ocean Park Blvd., Suite 200, Santa Monica, CA   90405
(310) 392-0522 • fax: (310) 392-8874
e-mail: admin@consumerwatchdog.org
Web site: www.consumerwatchdog.org

Consumer Watchdog (formerly the Foundation for Taxpayer and Consumer Rights) is a nationally recognized consumer group that has been fighting corporate and political corruption since 1985. Since its inception, Consumer Watchdog has worked to save Americans billions of dollars and improved countless peoples' lives by speaking out on behalf of consumers, including patients, rate payers, and policy holders. The organization's Web site publishes stories on a wide variety of topics, including financial regulation and credit scoring.

Federal Trade Commission (FTC)

Consumer Response Center, 600 Pennsylvania Ave. NW
Washington, DC   20580
(877) 382-4357
Web site: www.ftc.gov

The FTC is involved with issues that touch the economic life of every American. It is the only federal agency with both consumer protection and competition jurisdiction in broad sectors of the economy. The FTC pursues vigorous and effective law enforcement; advances consumers' interests by sharing its expertise with federal and state legislatures and U.S. and international government agencies; develops policy and research tools through hearings, workshops, and conferences; and creates practical and plain-language educational programs for consumers and businesses. The FTC's Web site offers information on a wide range of topics, including consumer protection, the Fair Debt Collection Practices Act, and credit and loans.

Truth About Credit
44 Winter St., Boston, MA   02108
(617) 747-4330
Web site: www.truthaboutcredit.org

Truth About Credit is a project of the U.S. PIRG (Public Interest Research Group) Education Fund and the Student PIRGs. U.S. PIRG pursues a mission of standing up to powerful interests on behalf of the public. U.S. PIRG conducts research, education, and advocacy on behalf of consumers. With the help of a professional staff of advocates and organizers, the Student PIRGs investigate problems and develop practical solutions and aim to convince the media and decision-makers to pay attention and take action on consumer protection and higher education issues. The organization's Web site features news stories about the perils of student credit card usage and highlights legislative news regarding the credit industry. Recent reports available on the Web site include *The Campus Credit Card Trap* and *Characteristics of Fair Campus Credit Cards.*

U.S. Department of Treasury
1500 Pennsylvania Ave. NW, Washington, DC   20220
(202) 622-2000 • fax: (202) 622-6415
Web site: www.ustreas.gov

The U.S. Treasury Department is the executive agency responsible for promoting economic prosperity and ensuring the financial security of the United States. The Department is responsible for a wide range of activities, including advising the president on economic and financial issues, encouraging sustainable economic growth, and fostering improved governance in financial institutions. The Treasury's Web site features recent financial news stories and links to numerous other consumer information sites. One such site, www.mymoney.gov, offers information about credit and financial planning for consumers, among other topics.

Bibliography

Books

Janet Bodnar
Raising Money Smart Kids: What They Need to Know About Money and How to Tell Them. Chicago: Dearborn Trade Publishing, 2005.

George Cooper
The Origin of Financial Crises: Central Banks, Credit Bubbles, and the Efficient Market Fallacy. New York: Vintage Books, 2008.

David S. Evans and Richard Schmalensee
Paying with Plastic: The Digital Revolution in Buying and Borrowing (2nd ed.). Cambridge, MA: MIT Press, 2005.

Joshua Holmberg
The Teen's Guide to Personal Finance: Basic Concepts in Personal Finance That Every Teen Should Know. Bloomington, IN: iUniverse, 2008.

Mary Hunt
Can I Pay My Credit Card Bill with a Credit Card?: And Other Financial Questions We're Too Embarrassed to Ask! Paramount, CA: DPL Press, 2009.

Tetsuya Ishikawa
How I Caused the Credit Crunch. London, UK: Icon Books Ltd., 2009.

Michael Mihalik   *Debt Is Slavery: And 9 Other Things I Wish My Dad Had Taught Me About Money.* Seattle, WA: October Mist, 2007.

J. Steve Miller   *Enjoy Your Money!: How to Make It, Save It, Invest It and Give It.* Acworth, GA: Wisdom Creek Press, 2009.

Jason R. Rich   *Dirty Little Secrets: What the Credit Bureaus Won't Tell You.* Irvine, CA: Entrepreneur Press, 2006.

James D. Scurlock   *Maxed Out: Hard Times in the Age of Easy Credit.* New York: Scribner, 2007.

Periodicals

Stephen Armstrong   "Drowning in Debt," *New Statesman*, June 2, 2008.

Susan Berfield   "Thirty and Broke," *Business Week*, November 14, 2005.

Erin Burt   "Just Say No to Credit Cards," *Kiplinger's Starting Out Web Column*, August 8, 2007.

M.P. Dunleavey   "How Teens Get Sucked into Credit Card Debt," *MSN Money*, May 31, 2006.

Lindsay Hesse   "In Recession, Students Cautious with Credit Cards," *The Brown and White*, February 3, 2009.

Yan Huang and Robert O. Weagley — "Sensation-seeking and College Students' Credit Card Debt," *Consumer Interests Annual*, vol. 53, 2007.

Dan Kaflec — "A Letter to My College-bound Daughter," *Money*, September 2008.

Michael Kinsman — "Debt-loaded Message," *San Diego Union-Tribune*, May 19, 2005.

Barbara Kiviat — "The Credit Crunch: Where Is It Happening?" *Time*, September 30, 2008.

Deanna Martin — "Should Schools Teach Kids About Personal Finance?" *Seattle Post-Intelligencer*, February 15, 2009.

Patrick McCormick — "B.A. in Bankruptcy," *U.S. Catholic*, July 2006.

Kimberly Palmer and Emily Brandon — "The Rush to Plastic," *U.S. News & World Report*, January 28, 2008.

Terrence Roche and Steve Williams — "The Fast and Fascinating Rise of Generation Y," *American Banker*, April 18, 2006.

Valerie Seckler — "Apparel Spending Is Up—So Is Debt," *WWD*, May 23, 2007.

Jenn Wiant — "Good Cents for Kids," *Northwest Herald*, February 11, 2009.

Index